table settings

table settings

stylish entertaining made simple

emily chalmers

with photography by David Brittain

RYLAND
PETERS
& SMALL

LONDON NEW YORK

First published in the United States in 2005
by Ryland Peters & Small
519 Broadway, 5th Floor
New York, NY 10012
www.rylandpeters.com

Senior designer Sally Powell
Senior editor Annabel Morgan
Picture research Emily Chalmers and
   Emily Westlake
Production Gemma Moules
Art director Gabriella Le Grazie
Publishing director Alison Starling

Stylist Emily Chalmers

The text and pictures in this book were first
published in *Table Inspirations* in 2001.

10 9 8 7 6 5 4 3 2 1

ISBN 1 84172 944 2

Library of Congress Cataloging-in-Publication Data

Chalmers, Emily.
  Table settings : stylish entertaining made simple / Emily Chalmers.-- 1st
ed.
      p. cm.
  ISBN 1-84172-944-2
  1. Table setting and decoration. 2. Entertaining. I. Title.
  TX879.C49 2005
  642'.6--dc22
                          2005003592

Printed and bound in China

6   introduction

the occasions

10   Lazy weekend breakfast
12   Indulgent brunch
14   Beach barbecue
16   Modern chic dining
18   Eating alfresco
20   Eastern-style banquet
22   Lunch on the lawn
24   Asian-style elegance
26   Cool classic dining
28   Romantic lunch for two
30   Father's Day spread
32   Mother's Day treat
34   Christening tea
36   Children's party
40   Surprise birthday buffet
42   Easter celebration
44   Rustic Halloween table
48   Exotic Christmas
50   New Year's Eve bash
52   Cocktails and canapés

the settings

55   International informal
56   British formal
57   English afternoon tea
58   American formal
59   French formal
60   Chinese informal
61   Japanese informal

62   sources
64   picture credits and
     acknowledgments

introduction

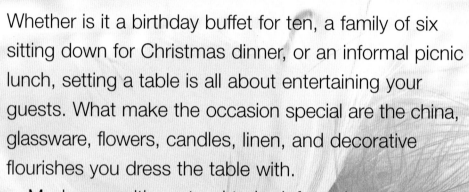

Whether is it a birthday buffet for ten, a family of six sitting down for Christmas dinner, or an informal picnic lunch, setting a table is all about entertaining your guests. What make the occasion special are the china, glassware, flowers, candles, linen, and decorative flourishes you dress the table with.

Modern mealtimes tend to be informal, so there is no need to feel confined by the "rules." A table can still look smart without sticking to the traditional silver flatware and linen napery, so long as it remains well considered and orderly. Flowers will add life and color to any table, as well as signaling that you are making an effort for your guests. Candles create intimacy and atmosphere. Place cards at each setting will make your guests feel special, yet, when you are pushed for time, these need only be squares of card stock dropped into empty wine glasses or wedged under a decorative pebble at the edge of each plate. And there are so many ways in which linen and flatware can be attractively displayed. It's the little details that make the difference. The table settings shown in this book are intended to inspire and excite you, so mix them with your own ideas and, most of all, have fun!

the occasions

There are many festive occasions that can inspire a special table setting, but sometimes it's just as enjoyable to make a celebration of an informal gathering with friends, or a quiet evening in at home. Take the occasion as the starting point for the table setting—for example, you could work with eggs at Easter, or use the rich colors of fall at Halloween. Equally, inspiration can stem from a bunch of your favorite flowers, a particular piece of fabric that you'd like to use on the table, or those new floating candles you're eager to experiment with.

left **Layer different-sized plates at each setting and serve yogurt and crunchy granola in tall, chunky glasses.**
opposite, above left **Offer a choice of different teas and coffees in labeled teapots.**
opposite, below left **Pack individual dishes with butter, chill them, then use a skewer to incise a name or initial to mark each place.**

A generous white tablecloth provides the foundation for this fresh and inviting breakfast table. Throw the cloth over your kitchen table and set it with the basic elements of a practical kitchen—chunky glassware and simple white china. Look out for dual-purpose tableware, too: if you are offering boiled eggs, why not try using your napkin rings as egg cups? Have fun with your settings. For example, you could personalize boiled eggs by writing your guests' names on the shell. Liven up the breakfast table with cheerful flowers in bold colors, like these bright sunflowers. Make sure there is tea and coffee on hand, and try not to fight over the newspapers!

lazy weekend breakfast

right **Bright flowers such as sunflowers or bold gerberas in tall jars are the perfect companions for a relaxed, sunny breakfast. Decant jelly and marmalade into small glass bowls or ramekins and pour fresh fruit juice into glass pitchers.**

An early morning meal needs an appealing setting that is worth getting out of bed for!

this page **A single orchid head looks wonderfully elegant nestling in a white china coffee cup.**

inset, below **Each place setting is carefully labeled and laid out in the same way. Create order before the chaos ensues!**

right **A place card in the form of a luggage label has been carefully tied to this orchid flower.**
below right **Here we see the table setting in its entirety, with all the elements—the flatware, china, glassware, flowers, and place cards—laid out neatly. The delicate cymbidium orchid and random scatterings of frosted-glass pebbles add a decorative touch that contrasts with the harder lines of the setting.**

indulgent brunch

A lavish brunch is the perfect way to spend a long, lazy Sunday morning. White china and stainless-steel flatware bring a clean, fresh look to the tabletop. Lay out glassware for water, juice, and Bloody Marys. A bowl of olives or nuts at each setting will provide guests with something to nibble on with a pre-brunch drink. Put cups and saucers at each place, so that everything is at hand. Finally, top each place setting with a bagel or muffin.

Cymbidium orchids are ideal for this sophisticated setting. They create a luxurious effect and a single stem goes a long way. Pluck off the orchid heads, and place each in a shot glass or tealight holder, before positioning one at each place setting. Small labels can be tied to each one if you want to use place cards.

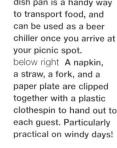

right A large aluminum dish pan is a handy way to transport food, and can be used as a beer chiller once you arrive at your picnic spot.
below right A napkin, a straw, a fork, and a paper plate are clipped together with a plastic clothespin to hand out to each guest. Particularly practical on windy days!

beach barbecue

If you're planning a cookout at the beach, invest in a disposable barbecue—it's by far the easiest option. If the meal is going to be a big event, set up a row of barbecues to cater for all those hungry mouths.

Paper plates and napkins are practical for picnics and barbecues, as they can all be thrown into a garbage bag at the end of the day. If it's windy, use clothespins to clip a napkin and utensil to each plate. Tin cups look good and are lightweight to carry. Pack plenty of cold meats, salads, dips, breads, and crunchy fruit. A dish pan can be used as an ice bucket to chill the drinks. Finally, take lanterns and cozy blankets for when the sun goes down.

left **A barbecue on the beach—what a treat! Take everything you need, so you are set up for the day. As well as plenty of delicious food and drink (including lots of bottled water), pack a few big blankets, a radio, and lots of reading material, as well as a football or Frisbee for the more energetic members of the party.** above **Breadsticks are bundled together with string, and a denim napkin has been rolled up and secured with twine and a shell.**

left and above This cool modern table setting is perfect for a lunchtime gathering. Settings are marked with placemats and a large platter holding a napkin. A centerpiece of artichoke heads makes a stylish impact. A bowl of exotic fruit could also work well; guests could then help themselves to dessert. Stick to a neutral color scheme—white china, plain flatware, and simple glassware complement natural materials like wood and slate.

Sticking to a neutral palette with dashes of gray and green and gleaming brushed metal creates a fresh and relaxed table setting for a funky dinner party, while the eye-catching centerpiece, floating candles, and glowing votives dotted around the table top remind guests that it is a special occasion.

right **A slab of slate acts as a condiment tray. The oil and vinegar have been decanted into recycled glass jars.**
below right **If you have chalk on hand, why not use the slate placemats to start an impromptu game between courses?**
below left **Floating candles in shallow dishes gently illuminate the corners of the table. A bamboo skewer is an inventive place-card holder, and the wedge of lime is both decorative and practical.**

modern chic dining

Sit candles in metallic holders, and use a galvanized tin to hold the centerpiece. Foliage or vegetables look more modern than flowers. Try interesting shapes, such as knobbly gourds or artichoke heads.

Keep things simple—lay each place with a placemat, the basic flatware, a large platter, and a napkin. Slate placemats double up as blackboards. Chalk on your guests' names, or use the slate for games. Keep glassware simple, but be inventive with place cards. Spike them onto bamboo skewers or cocktail sticks and pop them in a glass.

eating alfresco

You don't need a large garden for open-air dining. Any outdoor space will do, as long as there is enough room for a table! If you don't have any garden furniture, try a sturdy wallpapering table and conceal it under a cloth. Stick to a color scheme of strong Mediterranean tones, using white and blue with splashes of bright pink. The glassware and crockery should be sturdy and chunky. Even if it's daylight, it always makes it special to have candles on the table. Lanterns are fun, too, when dining out doors—hang them from branches or fencing. Put candles in glass holders and surround them with petals, chips of colored glass, or colored sand (available from pet shops and aquatic suppliers).

Prepare an alfresco lunch on the terrace, combining deep blue with a white backdrop and accents of shocking-pink bougainvillea.

Be experimental with color for an elegant, sophisticated Eastern-themed dinner party. Find a sumptuous piece of fabric to use as a runner or tablecloth, and choose napkins that will work well with it. Experiment with folding them in different ways, or try placing them under the plates. Next, position a row of plants along the center of the table.

eastern-style banquet

If possible, put them in bowls that tie in with the dinner service you are using. Orchids are ideal for an Eastern theme: their roots are reasonably shallow and the plants can be easily transferred and reused in other settings. Colored glassware such as pretty antique cut glass works well with this theme. Scour antique stores and flea markets for interesting pieces. Don't worry if you only find single glasses, as they can be used as unusual tealight holders or mixed with other odd pieces for a quirky bohemian look.

opposite **This length of unusual fabric makes a great runner and provided the inspiration for an Asian-inspired table setting.**
above and right **Mix up materials around the table. Silvered-glass cups, dull metal flatware, and glossy earthenware dishes create an interesting effect that brings everything together. Slender orchids won't block the view across the table or interrupt conversation.**

lunch on the lawn

Taking your lunch out onto the lawn is always a special treat, and even a simple salad benefits from an idyllic garden setting. Keep the color scheme simple and uncomplicated, using neutrals and shades of white, and take inspiration from the surroundings when choosing flowers and tableware, picking delicately colored flowerheads and using grasses to tie around napkins and cups.

Soften a metal garden table with a piece of fabric for a floaty, leisurely look. Linen would be the perfect fabric for both tablecloth and napkins, but bleached denim or unbleached cotton muslin look equally good, and are an inexpensive way to conceal a weathered garden table. Set each place with a large dish and a single fork. Fold the napkins down to coaster size and place them under cups. Choose thick chunky glass, preferably recycled, and either decant your drinks or stick to attractive spring-water bottles.

opposite, below left and right **A soapstone vase is used as a water cooler. Soapstone's natural insulating properties will keep drinks cool on a hot day. Decorative feather butterflies perch on the edge of each wine glass.**
opposite, above **A strand of bear grass has been tied around each chunky cup for a decorative touch. A plain linen napkin has been folded and tucked beneath the cup.**
above **A couple of soft pink garden blooms add delicate spots of color to this understated table.**
right **A simple setting like this can be put together in a few minutes. Combine lots of natural materials, such as linen, soapstone, and recycled glass.**

Don't worry if you don't have a dining table; a low surface, such as a coffee table, is the ideal starting point for an Asian-style meal.

opposite **The strong, graphic lines so typical of Asian interiors are here softened with the addition of small candles, floating flowerheads, and bowls of tasty Oriental nibbles.**

asian-style elegance

Eating at a low level, seated on cushions, will give any meal a decadent, intimate feel. Use heavy linen or a long raffia mat to cover the tabletop. Choose tableware in simple shapes and a muted palette, and add splashes of color with flowers. Pull up a bench to stack any china necessary for the following courses—this will help keep the tabletop clean and uncluttered. Have a good rummage around Asian food stores for individual bottles of drink to put in place of glasses at each setting. Fun packages of fruit juice can be found, and cute miniature bottles of saki will also fit the theme.

above left **Stick to the basics—a noodle bowl, napkin, and chopsticks—at each place.**
above right **With their delicate form and strong magenta hue, Singapore orchids relieve the subdued colors of the table setting.**
right **Create a centerpiece from a large dish or tray holding bowls of unusual pickles and relishes, and bottles of soy sauce and sesame oil for guests to help themselves to.**

left **Warm candlelight casts a magical glow that extends over the mantelpiece and sideboard, combining with the soft fern fronds to bring a subtle elegance to the occasion. Between the lines of white linen, rows of hollow glass baubles have been interspersed with tealights, accentuating the glowing spots of light. This is a very graphic setting, with lots of circular objects set out in orderly lines. The minimal fern fronds give it a hint of softness; cool white calla lilies would have fitted in well here, too.**

It's always a pleasure to have the chance to do something special with table settings, and a formal dinner offers the perfect opportunity. If you are using your everyday table, smarten it up with a starched white tablecloth or placemats. If you have neither of these, then use well-ironed white napkins to mark each place.

It's the abundance of sparkling glassware that gives this table its elegant, sophisticated feel. Candles also create a festive effect. Small metal-cased tealights are ideal, and can be dotted around the table. Look out for plain-glass votive holders, too, to add to the minimal feel. Arrange fragile glass droplets or hollow baubles between the candles, or cluster them together in glass bowls.

Flowers and foliage can be most effective when they are kept to a minimum. Here, a frond of fern in a simple low vase serves to accentuate the minimal look.

cool classic dining

left A beaded napkin ring is a decadent place-card holder.
below A plain-glass dip tray found at a thrift store makes an excellent dish for nibbles.
right Well-starched linen placemats lie across the table, while matching napkins sit along the back of each chair.

Choose classic simple shapes for stylish elegance and keep everything to a minimum.

above **One way to bring color and texture to the table is to tie flatware or chopsticks together. Try thick strands of grass or clusters of feathers with a wired malleable end. Or thread beads or buttons onto wire and twist it around the stems of your glassware.**
right **This bright studio apartment scrubs up well for a romantic meal. Red and green work well together and the color** theme is repeated in the glassware, china, and flowers. Even the candles are displayed in tealight holders that tie in with the fiery red and muted green scheme.
opposite, above **Tealight holders have been put into service as individual salt and pepper holders.**
opposite, below **A card holder is a fun way to present place cards as well as old photographs of the two of you.**

A romantic table setting makes a low-key Saturday lunchtime into a special occasion. The obvious dates are Valentine's Day or an anniversary, but this table is also easy to put together for a birthday or other celebration.

romantic lunch for two

Red is the traditional color for romantic liaisons, and here it adds spice and depth to the khaki ceramics. Jazz up the setting with bold red napkins and glossy red chopsticks. Cacti and grasses make unusual funky centerpieces; if you're not opting for red roses, that is! Plants look fabulous in glass bowls on beds of white gravel or stones, and miniature Christmas tree lights can be twisted onto plants to provide additional sparkle. As well as candles and flowers, decorate the tabletop with little gifts or mementoes. Dig out photos of special times, or set indulgent chocolates or exotic drinks at both places. Try brightly colored drinks, such as Campari, or add grenadine to wine or sparking water for more color.

left **A bundle of bamboo stalks knotted together with a strand of bear grass decorates each place setting. Place cards and an individual salt shaker are popped into the side bowls.**
below left **A chunky glass tank vase makes an ideal vessel for a selection of olives.**
below right **Metal, glass, and the rich tints of red wine harmonize beautifully together.**

Father's Day offers the opportunity to set the table in a chic, masculine style that would also be suitable for a formal occasion such as a business lunch. Here, dark-hued china is teamed with colorful glassware, creating an exotic yet contemporary effect. A glass-topped table is an excellent base for different textures and colors, and a linen

father's day spread

runner will soften and protect the tabletop, as will tablemats and coasters. Leather and felt can both be cut into mats—add interest by using pinking shears around the edges. Flatware should be plain and simple, with the minimum number of utensils on the table. To continue the pared-down effect, two wine tumblers are stacked at each place, with a water glass to one side. The strong colors are further enhanced by glass votive holders wrapped in richly colored handmade paper. Choose a bold, sculptural centerpiece, such as pussy willow and bamboo in a tall vase.

above **A plain-glass votive holder has been wrapped with a piece of Oriental paper to cast a rich glow that livens up the surrounding glass elements.**

right **The clean lines of this classic glass table and the leather chairs provide a great foundation for a Father's Day spread. Colors have been kept subdued and darkly masculine, with stoneware plates, terracotta and ochre napkins, and gray felt mats and coasters. The zingy yellow glassware brings a touch of spice to the proceedings.**

this page and inset, right
**Good-quality silverware is laid
out beside a pretty bobble-edged
glass plate all ready for lunch.
Each place setting is adorned
with its own miniature bouquet,
for the guests to take home with
them as a party favor.**

right and below right **The gentle pastel notes of the flowers and table linen, along with the dainty pieces of glassware, make this an excellent setting for a Mother's Day lunch. Softly colored glass tumblers and Moroccan tea glasses only enhance the scheme, while a bottle of green tea with dainty Oriental-style packaging sits happily alongside the other elements.**

mother's day treat

Flowers are a good starting point for a Mother's Day lunch. Base your table on soft shades inspired by sweet peas, pansies, and peonies. A Mother's Day meal offers the perfect opportunity to bring out all your prettiest things, such as dainty glass plates and Moroccan tea glasses. Mix and match these at each place setting and use them to serve the food on. Subtle silver or clear acrylic-handled flatware works well in this setting, as do pastel napkins in a similarly soft hue. Scour your local delicatessen or patisserie for delicious cream cakes or petits fours, and set them on a delicate glass or china cakestand at the center of the tabletop. For added sparkle, surround the centerpiece with a ring of tealights in glass holders. And be inventive with flowers, placing a bijou arrangement of cottage-garden flowers at each place.

christening tea

Welcoming a new baby into the world is a wonderful excuse for a celebration. For a small gathering lay an informal table in the kitchen, but if you are expecting a lot of visitors opt for a themed buffet table instead.

Stick to clear pastel pinks and blues. Cotton gingham is fresh and pretty, used as simple runners lying across the width of the table. Continuing the theme, plain napkins have been tied with gingham ribbon. If you have any pastel-colored china, now is the chance to use it. Pink candles and bonbons continue the pastel decorative theme and, for a dainty flower display, simple glass vases hold single pink roses, lisianthus, and eucalyptus.

this page **Chunky water glasses between each setting hold fluffy white marshmallows and pink sugared almonds.**
inset, left **The candies bring additional interest to the table and match the baby-blue and palest-pink colour scheme perfectly. A piece of pink gingham ribbon tied around each napkin provides a dainty finishing touch.**

opposite **A string of tree lights adorned with artificial flowers will liven up the party table.**
right **Clear lemonade can be jazzed up with the addition of a splash of food coloring.**
far right **Toy goldfish swimming in a large plastic bowl make an irresistible centerpiece.**
below right **If you have time, why not personalize each setting with a Polaroid photograph (taken as each guest arrives) clipped to each bowl.**

children's party

When it comes to children's parties, think bright, bold, and cheerful. This is one occasion where you can let your imagination run riot. The kitchen is an ideal setting. Spills won't matter too much, and everything is at hand for serving and clearing up.

Opt for a zingy color scheme with lots of juicy clashing shades. Make each child a placemat from felt, bright carpet remnants, or Astroturf for a surreal effect that kids will love. Peel the labels off clear plastic bottles and fill them with colorful drinks. Place a glass or metal bowl at each place (a mixing bowl is ideal) and pile it with goodies—a metal lunchbox containing tiny sandwiches, chips, and mini-muffins, and pieces of dried fruit and

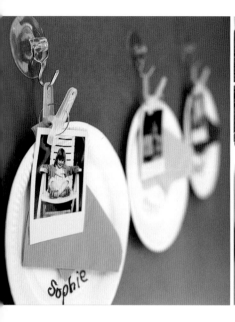

far left **Hang paper plates and napkins along the wall**, right at hand for when the birthday cake comes out.
left **Display bright flowers**, such as sunflowers or gerberas, in water or milk bottles.
below **If you want to protect your table**, invest in a paper tablecloth and leave out lots of crayons to draw with.
inset, right **A string of twinkling tree lights** set among shocking-pink artificial flowers bring added sparkle to the table setting.

Stick to a palette of bright primary colors for the maximum "wow" factor.

other treats all wrapped and tied with string. Kids will love opening their "presents" and devouring the contents! For dessert, serve wobbly jello in lots of wild colors.

Decorate the table with zany toys—rubber frogs and goldfish and colorful parrots perched on the chair backs. Other quirky ideas include funky Christmas-tree lights running down the center of the table and jolly gerberas set in milk bottles. If you cover your table with a white paper cloth, you can set out cups of crayons and encourage each little guest to discover their inner artist!

right **Each place setting is crowded with colorful things to eat, drink, and play with—perfect to tempt young partygoers. Plastic toys, a bowl of jello, jewel-colored soft drinks, a wacky square of grass, and a host of irresistible candy-colored packages turn the party table into a wonderland!**

above **Edible flower petals have been frozen in ice for a pretty, colorful effect.**

left **Anything goes, as long as it's pink! A string of fuchsia-pink Chinese paper lanterns sets the color theme for this party, while a line of berry-colored vodka jellos sits along the window ledge. The cartons of guava juice were chosen for their kitsch pink packaging.**

opposite, above **A large tealight sits inside a group of bangles.**

opposite, below **Single birthday candles have been placed in meringues so everyone gets a birthday wish!**

opposite, below right **Clear-glass tank vases hold both food and decorations. The candles can be lit just before the party kicks off.**

surprise
birthday buffet

This birthday buffet spread has a kitsch, girly theme. We chose food, candles, and tableware to fit the flamingo-pink color scheme, and went to town with decorative touches, such as feathers and artificial flowers. For food in the palest pink shades, make colored ice cubes and add a dash of scarlet food coloring to meringue mix and frosting. Decorate everyday glassware or plastic cups with stick-on glittery bindis or transfers to fit the theme. Stand candles in jam jars or glass tank vases, and decorate the area around the buffet table with hanging paper lanterns and twinkling tree lights. Garlands of paper flowers add to the feminine glamour.

left **Two different sets of plates have been used and their arrangement is alternated at each place.**
below left **These eggs have been blown, then painted in pastel shades. On a bed of silk and feathers, they make a decorative centerpiece.**
below **Incorporate feathers into the setting, such as the mini feather dusters popped in each glass and the feather "nests" at each place.**

Easter Sunday is a good day for a special lunch with family or friends. It also offers a good opportunity for a fun table setting. A palette of delicate pastels—pale pink, green, and blue—enlivened with bold pink is perfect for this occasion. Enjoy playing with texture, combining chalky matte eggshells, fine linen, and soft feathers.

easter celebration

The foundation is a pale linen runner or cloth. A complete set of matching china is not essential—use differently patterned china in similar tones. For a centerpiece, buy small tester pots of chalky pastel-colored paint, and paint hard-boiled eggs. Arrange them in small bowls and individual egg cups. Continue the theme with the individual settings, creating "nests" at each place and providing chocolate eggs to nibble on before the main meal is served. The witty touches, such as fluffy feathers and chocolate eggs, will appeal to guests, young and old alike.

above Instead of formal place cards, use ribbon to tie an old-fashioned luggage label to the back of each chair.

right French windows lead to the garden to allow for a quick Easter egg hunt after lunch! The surrounding areas—the side table and sofa—have been decorated in the same dreamy pastel color scheme as the dining-room table.

Try something a little different for Halloween and decorate a humble kitchen table with the fruits and colors of the season.

opposite **Wooden dishes and bowls hold groups of vegetables for display and nuts for guests to nibble on between courses. This rich, abundant setting presents a wonderful still-life effect at each place, combining lacquered chopsticks with artichokes and miniature gourds.**

rustic halloween table

Get inspired by the colors of fall—mustard, amber, reds, and greens—and create a setting for a Halloween meal. Base your theme around seasonal fruits and vegetables—gourds, squashes, artichokes, and satsumas all work well with the more traditional choice of pumpkins.

Enjoy the varied textures of the fruit and vegetables and try to reflect this in your setting. If you have chunky ceramic bowls and plates in warm tones, now is the time to bring them out. Unify the spread by sitting each bowl upon a wood or rattan lay plate or charger, or a placemat. Build up layers of

above left **The table's centerpiece is an aged wooden bowl piled high with gourds and pumpkins heaped around a central candle.** above right **Wooden bowls look great on a warmly colored tablecloth—perfect for a Halloween meal.** right **Everything on the table—placemats, bowls, flatware—echoes the rich shades of fall.**

Choose candles in rich fall shades to make sure everything is glowing.

color and don't be afraid to use large fabric placemats with smaller mats on top—it will look fabulous once the table is fully laid. Think about your choice of flatware. There are many suitable styles, including those with handles made of bamboo, wood, colorful resin, and so on. Alternatively, jazz up basic steel flatware by tying a jaunty bow on the handles. Glassware in shades of red, green, and yellow works well on this table. Find beer and water bottles with interesting shapes and labels. Choose candles in rich fall shades and make sure everything is glowing for a true Halloween experience. Multicolored tree lights will also encourage the festive spirit.

above and right **As the evening draws in and the room grows dark, the richly dressed table will become even more colorful, with the string of glowing chile lights and the abundance of different-sized candles.**

left **You don't have to have a Christmas tree— just decorate any suitable houseplants.**
below left **Richly colored candles, chocolate coins, and fruit combine to make this a really festive setting.**
below right **Old wine glasses hold small candles set in decorative red sand and glitter.**
opposite **Suspend baubles on ribbon or cord from a centrally positioned light fixture.**

Red, gold, and green are the traditional colors of Christmas, but here they've been employed in more unexpected ways for an exotic festive table. Banana leaves from an Oriental supermarket are the table covering for this setting. Bold and beautiful flowers continue the theme—orchids or dramatic

exotic christmas

amaryllis would both be perfect. Candles will intensify the warmth and festivity of the occasion—sit them on thick candlesticks or old wine glasses. Give any odd saucers or candleholders a makeover with a quick blast of gold spray paint. Little gifts are presented in bags made from metallic organza at each place. Be creative with your decorations. Forget the tree and dangle them from light fixtures, door knobs, and picture rails. The decorations don't have to be traditional— you could hang foil-wrapped chocolates and fortune cookies for an unexpected twist.

opposite **Chocolates sit on a bed of Cellophane for a magical touch.**
opposite, inset **Knives and forks are popped into silvery mailing bags.**
right **Each setting has a cool, frosty glamour, from the central runner made from metallic giftwrap to the arctic-blue shot glasses.**
below **Blue and silver have been rigidly adhered to in order to create a space-age feel.**
below right **Sit candles in little jars of glitter for a festive display.**

Silver is always a good color for New Year's Eve, especially if you enjoyed a surfeit of gold at Christmas. Choose one other color to go with the silver—pink or blue will work well—and stick to these two colors. Play around with different materials. Instead of

new year's eve bash

opting for your usual dinner plates, be funky with metal pie plates and foil take-out containers. Cover cake bases with aluminum foil and use them as tablemats or lay plates. Iridescent glitter, tree lights, Cellophane, and silver paper can all be used to decorate the tabletop and the surrounding area.

Choose flowers that sit well within your chosen color scheme. You can buy dyed carnations, or can spray white carnations with silver paint for a space-age effect. For an alternative centerpiece, float flowerheads in a bowl surrounded by floating candles.

opposite **Everything is laid out on a circular table to allow maximum access. The rich stained-glass colors and chic, sophisticated glassware create a glamorous, indulgent effect.**
below **The table is scattered with special decorative touches, such as the feather butterflies on wire that have been used to bind together the flatware. The rich jewel colors are echoed in the choice of food.**

cocktails and canapés

above left **Each food offering has been decorated with candles, pebbles, and leaves—chic and dramatic, yet relatively inexpensive.**
above right **An elegant cocktail shaker is a practical and decorative necessity for this occasion. Glasses and tumblers have been decorated with fun metallic party pieces, such as streamers and miniature glitter balls. A bead curtain provides a glam backdrop.**

A cocktail party is fun to plan for a birthday or New Year's Eve celebration, or is a good way to liven up an ordinary Saturday night! Plan a buffet spread and theme everything from flatware to drinks. Here, it really is the presentation that counts, so take your cue from professional caterers and decorate trays of canapés with nightlights and pebbles and serve up the food on glossy banana leaves. Keep an eye out for decorations on wire and use them to wrap around knives and forks. When it comes to color, take brightly colored liqueurs and mixers as your inspiration, with candles in rich jewellike blues, greens, and reds. Shake up a few cocktails, and the party will be well under way!

A stylish cocktail party is fun for a birthday or New Year's Eve celebration, or is a good way to liven up an ordinary Saturday night!

the settings

Modern mealtimes tend to be rather informal, but there are occasions when a more formal setting is called for. A table laid with row upon row of eating implements can seem daunting, but this need not be the case. Provided the table is laid correctly and you follow the simple rule of using the outermost utensils first, you can't go wrong. A thoughtful host will lay the table carefully for a formal meal, so that no guest need feel embarrassed by making a mistake.

international informal

The most common setting for an informal Western meal positions the dinner knife to the right of the dinner plate, with the soup spoon to the right of the knife. The dinner fork is positioned to the left of the plate, with the napkin neatly folded to the left of the fork. The dessert fork and spoon are then laid horizontally above the plate, the fork first, with the handle pointing to the left, and the spoon above it, with the handle pointing to the right.

1	Napkin in a simple fold	6	Dessert fork
2	Dinner fork	7	Dessert spoon
3	Dinner plate	8	White wine glass
4	Dinner knife	9	Red wine glass
5	Soup spoon	10	Water glass

British formal

A formal meal provides an opportunity to use lots of china and flatware. If you have a large dining-room table, make full use of the space by laying the dessert spoon and fork inside the dinner knife and fork, and by including a butter plate to the left of the setting. The dinner knife and fork are used together in the European style, with the fork held in the left hand, tines down, and the knife held in the right hand for cutting and for guiding food onto the fork.

1 Napkin in a simple fold
2 Butter plate
3 Dinner fork
4 Dessert fork
5 Dinner plate
6 Dessert spoon
7 Dinner knife
8 Soup spoon
9 White wine glass
10 Red wine glass
11 Water glass

English afternoon tea

For afternoon tea, the butter plate is placed centrally, with a napkin positioned to the left, and the bread knife, pudding spoon, and pie fork (in that order) positioned to the right-hand side of the butter plate. The teacup and saucer are set above the flatware, with the teaspoon lying horizontally on the saucer behind the cup. The teacup handle should be sitting parallel to the teaspoon.

1 Napkin in a simple fold
2 Butter plate
3 Bread knife
4 Dessert spoon
5 Pie fork

6 Saucer
7 Teacup
8 Teaspoon

American formal

This formal setting is for a three-course meal with a fish appetizer. A bread knife is optional, and would be laid on the butter plate. When eating the main course, the dinner fork is transferred to the right hand for each bite, and back to the left hand when the knife is required for cutting. Dessert utensils can also be laid across the top of the setting or brought in when dessert is served. It is not necessary to use both spoon and fork, but it may be easier.

1 Napkin in a simple fold
2 Fish fork
3 Dinner fork
4 Dessert fork
5 Dinner plate
6 Dessert spoon
7 Dinner knife
8 Fish knife
9 White wine glass
10 Red wine glass
11 Water glass
12 Butter plate

French formal

French settings differ from American and British in a number of ways. Butter plates and knives are not used, as bread is laid directly onto the table and butter is not served. Forks and spoons rest face down and a tablespoon is used in favor of the more familiar, rounded soup spoon. A knife rest is required so that the dinner knife can be laid back on the table, ready to be used for the cheese course, before dessert is served.

1 Napkin in a simple fold	6 Dinner knife
2 Dinner fork	7 Soup spoon
3 Dessert fork	8 White wine glass
4 Dinner plate	9 Red wine glass
5 Dessert spoon	10 Water glass

Chinese informal

For a Chinese meal, the chopsticks should be laid together to the right of the dinner plate, with the ends resting on a stand. The soup bowl and teacup are laid behind the plate, and a small dish for sauce is placed in front of the teacup. The soup spoon may be positioned in the bowl or at the side, to the left of the chopsticks. It is polite to offer guests who may be inexperienced with chopsticks the option of a knife and fork.

1 Dinner plate
2 Chopsticks
3 Chopstick stand
4 Sauce dish
5 Teacup
6 Soup bowl
7 Soup spoon
8 Saucer

Japanese informal

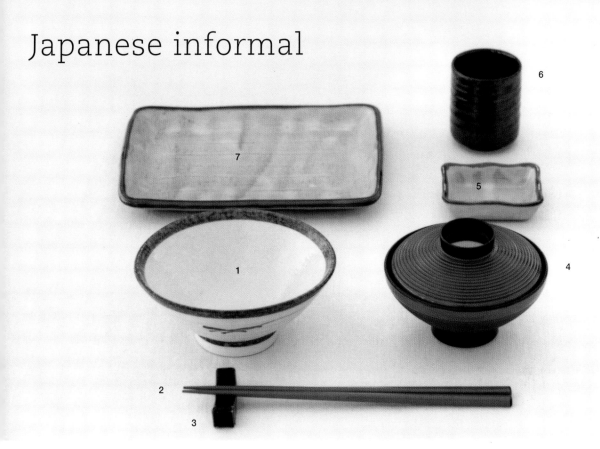

There are many possible settings for a Japanese meal, depending upon the occasion and the food being served. For a basic setting, the rice bowl is on the left and the lidded soup bowl on the right. Fried or grilled foods are served in an open plate behind the rice bowl, with a small dish for relish at the side. A cup for tea sits at the back on the right. Chopsticks lie horizontally resting side by side on a stand at the front, pointing to the left.

1 Rice bowl
2 Chopsticks
3 Chopstick stand
4 Soup bowl
5 Relish dish
6 Teacup
7 Dinner plate

sources

CHINA AND TABLEWARE

ABC Carpet & Home
888 Broadway
New York, NY 10003
For a store near you, call
(212) 473-3000 or visit
www.abchome.com
New and vintage linens,
silverware, crystal,
tableware, dinnerware,
fabrics, and trim.

Anthropologie
375 West Broadway
New York, NY 10012
(212) 343-7070
For a store near you, call
(800) 309-2500 or visit
www.anthropologie.com
Pretty tableware and
vintage-inspired linens.

Bed, Bath & Beyond
For a store near you, call
1-800-GOBEYOND or visit
www.bedbathandbeyond.com
Linens, kitchenware,
candles, and glassware.

Christofle
680 Madison Avenue
New York, NY 10022
(212) 308-9390
www.christofle.com
Top-of-the-line French
crystal and china.

Corning/Revere
For a retailer near you, call
1-800-999-3436 or visit
www.corningware.com
Ceramic dishes for oven
and table.

The Conran Shop
407 East 59th Street
New York, NY 10022
(212) 755-9079
www.conran.com
Stylish home furnishings,
vases, and kitchenware.

Crate & Barrel
1860 W. Jefferson
Naperville, IL 60540
For a store near you, call
(800) 967-6696 or visit
www.crateandbarrel.com
Kitchenware, glassware,
china, and linens.

Dansk
For a retailer near you, call
(800) BY-DANSK or visit
www.dansk.com
Stylish modern glassware,
flatware, and dinnerware

Denby Pottery Co. Ltd.
For a retailer near you, call
(800) DENBY-4U or visit
www.denbyusa.com
Chunky tableware in
sophisticated hues.

Fishs Eddy
889 Broadway
New York, NY 10003
(212) 420-9020
For a store near you, call
(877) 347 4733 or visit
www.fishseddy.com
Funky, inexpensive china
and colored glassware.

Global Table
109 Sullivan Street
New York, NY 10012
(212) 431-5839
www.globaltable.com
Exotic tableware, dishes,
glassware, flatware, sake
sets, and unusual candles.

Lenox
For a retailer near you, call
(800) 63-LENOX or visit
www.lenox.com
Fine china, stemware,
flatware, and table linen.

Mikasa
For a retailer near you, call
(800) 866-MIKASA1 or visit
www.mikasa.com
Good quality, reasonably
priced dinnerware, crystal,
and flatware.

Moss
146 Greene Street
New York, NY 10012
(212) 226-2190
www.mossonline.com
Chic contemporary
glassware and housewares.

Pfaltzgraff
For mail order or a
retailer near you, call
(800) 999-2811 or visit
www.pfaltzgraff.com
Casual dinnerware and
home accessories.

Pier 1 Imports
461 Fifth Avenue
New York, NY 10017
For a store near you, call
(800) 245-4595 or visit
www.pier1.com
Baskets, candles,
candleholders, table linen,
dinnerware, glassware, and
home decor items.

Platypus
126 Spring Street
New York, NY 10012
(212) 219-3919
Eclectic kitchenware, china,
glassware, and flatware.

Pottery Barn
For your nearest store call
1-888-779-5179 or visit
www.potterybarn.com
Stylish, well-priced tabletop
essentials.

Quong Yuen Shin & Co.
32 Mott Street
New York, NY 10002
(212) 962-6280
Chinese tea sets, rice
bowls, and plates.

Reed & Barton
For a retailer near you, call
(800) 343-1383 or visit
www.reedandbarton.com
Silverware in modern and
traditional styles.

Restoration Hardware
For a store near you, call
(800) 816-0969 or visit
www.restorationhardware.com
Stylish barware, novelty
plates, coasters and
napkins, and table decor.

Tiffany & Co.
Fifth Avenue at 57th Street
New York, NY 10022
For a store near you, call
(800) 843-3269 or visit
www.tiffany.com
Elegant candlesticks, vases,
dinnerware, and crystal.

Wallace Silversmiths
For a retailer near you, call
(617) 561-2200 or visit
www.wallacesilver.com
Sterling silver and stainless
steel flatware.

Williams-Sonoma
51 Highland Park Village
Dallas Highland
Dallas, TX 75205
For a store near you, call
(800) 541-2233 or visit
www.williamssonoma.com
Glassware, barware,
flatware, cookware, linens,
and decorative accents.

TABLE LINENS

Laura Ashley
398 Columbus Avenue
New York, NY 10024-5105
(212) 496-5110
www.lauraashley.com
Tablecloths, napkins, and
fabric by the yard.

**Domenica Rosa Fine
Linens & Accessories**
12016 Poppy Street N.W.
Minneapolis, MN 55433
(888) 354-9388
www.domenicarosa.com
Tablecloths and tablecloths
in every color.

Fine Linens
1193 Lexington Avenue
New York, NY 10028
(212) 737-2123
www.finelinens.com
Linen placemats and
matching napkins.

Gumps
135 Post Street
San Francisco, CA 94108
Call (800) 882-8055 or visit
www.gumps.com
Silk table runners and
decorative placemats.

The Linen Closet Online
Call (800) 561-7331 or visit
www.thelinenclosetonline.com
Yves Delorme fine French
table linen and Xochi
placemats in many colors.

Peacock Alley
3210 Armstrong Avenue
Dallas, TX 75205
(214) 520-6736
www.peacockalley.com
Fine table linens.

CANDLES

Chandlers Candle
For mail order, call
(800) 463-7143 or visit
www.chandlerscandle.com
Chic bamboo-look pillar
candles.

Covington Candle
976 Lexington Avenue
New York, NY 10021
(212) 472-1131
Dinner and pillar candles in
various colors and sizes.

Illuminations
1995 South McDowell
Boulevard
Petaluma, CA 94954
For a store near you call
1-800-621-2998 or visit
www.illuminations.com
Candles and candle
accessories.

Yankee Candle Co.
South Deerfield, MA 01373
For a retailer near you, call
(877) 803-6890 or visit
www.yankeecandle.com
Decorative candles, votives,
and candleholders.

**DECORATIVE PAPERS,
RIBBONS, FLOWERS,
AND ACCESSORIES**

B & J Florist Supplies
103 West 28th Street
New York, NY 10001
(212) 564-6086
Florist supplies, including
fabric ribbon and simple
ornaments on wire ends.

Bill's Flower Market Inc.
816 Sixth Avenue
New York, NY 10001
(212) 889-8154
www.billsflowermarket.com
Artificial birds, colored
sand, feathers, and flowers.

Cape Cod Crafters
Route 1
Kittery, ME 04032
For a store near you visit
www.capecodcrafters.com
Ribbons, candles, and
table decorations.

Carlson Craft
1750 Tower Boulevard
North Mankato, MN 56003
(800) 774-6848
www.carlsoncraft.com
Party invitations.

Crane & Co.
30 South Street
Dalton, MA 01226
(413) 684-2600
www.crane.com
Invitations for all occasions.

Jam Paper
111 Third Avenue
New York, NY 10003
For details of their other
stores, call (212) 473-6666
or visit www.jampaper.com
Specialty paper, ribbons,
and packaging.

Kate's Paperie
140 W 57th St
New York, NY
(212) 459-0700
www.katespaperie.com
Ribbons, boxes, and bags.

M&J Trimmings
www.mjtrim.com
Sequined flowers, ribbon,
lace, rosettes, and
rhinestones.

Pearl River
www.pearlriver.com
Colorful and affordable
Chinese imports, from
paper decorations and
lacquered chopsticks to
quirky candies and satin
pincushions.

The Ribbonerie
191 Potrero Avenue
San Francisco, CA 94103
(415) 626-6184
www.theribbonerie.com
Unusual ribbons from
around the world.

Snow & Graham
For a retailer near you, call
(773) 665-9000 or visit
www.snowandgraham.com
Funky, modern invitations.

The Sweet Palace
109 East Broadway
Philipsburg, MT 59858
(888) 793-3896
www.sweetpalace.com
Old-fashioned candies and
suckers to buy online. Will
appeal to any kid!

architects and designers whose work is featured in this book

Elizabeth Blank
Floral & Interior Designer
77 Regent's Park Road
London NW1 8UY
+44 20 7722 1066
Pages: 32–33

TAG Architects
14 Belsize Crescent
London NW3 5QU
+44 20 7431 7974
www.tag-architects.co.uk
Pages: 48–49

Robert Dye Associates
Design Consultants/Chartered
Architects
Linton House
39–51 Highgate Road
London NW5 1RS
+44 20 7267 9388
fax 020 7267 9345
info@robertdye.com
www.robertdye.com
Pages: 36–39

MOOArc
198 Blackstock Road
London N5 1EN
+44 20 7354 1729
www.mooarc.com
Pages: 12–13

Levitt Bernstein Architects
1 Kingsland Passage
London E8 2BB
+44 20 7275 7676
fax +44 20 7275 9348
www.levittbernstein.co.uk
Pages: 2–3, 16–17

picture credits

Page **2–3** Aggie Mackenzie's kitchen in north London designed by Matthew Goulcher & Levitt Bernstein, built by LAD Construction; **9** Ros Fairman's house in London; **10–11** Sophy Hoare's house in London; **12–13** the Rowlands family's house in London designed by MOOArc; **16–17** Aggie Mackenzie's kitchen in north London designed by Matthew Goulcher & Levitt Bernstein, built by LAD Construction; **18–19** Clare Mannix-Andrews's house in Hove; **22–23** Ros Fairman's house in London; **24–25** Clare Mannix-Andrews's house in Hove; **26–27** Marian Cotterill's house in London; **30–31** Stephan Schulte's apartment at York Central in London; **32–33** an apartment in London designed by Elizabeth Blank; **34–35** Marian Cotterill's house in London; **36–39** Robert and Lucinda Dye's house in London designed by Robert Dye Associates; **42–43** Marian Cotterill's house in London; **44–47** Sophy Hoare's house in London; **48–49** house in Hampstead designed by TAG Architects; **52–3** Stephan Schulte's apartment at York Central in London.

acknowledgments

First and foremost I would like to say thank you to David Brittain for his incredible and unfailing visual talent, support, and friendship. Thanks also to Marc Kirk, who kept us laughing, and to Catherine Griffin for lots of things, including her fantastic design skills and dedication.

Thanks to Debi Treloar and Louise Leffler for introducing me to Ryland Peters & Small, and to Gabriella Le Grazie for giving me such an enjoyable and inspiring opportunity. Finally, thanks to Sophie Bevan for her wonderful way with words.